FOOD FROM THE SHORE

FOOD FROM THE SHORE

Nat Gordon

ADAM & CHARLES BLACK
LONDON

First published 1980
A & C Black (Publishers) Ltd.
35 Bedford Row, London WC1R 4JH

© 1980 Nat Gordon

ISBN 0 7136 2059 5

Gordon, Nat
 Food from the seashore.
 1. Cookery (Sea food)
 2. Cookery, English
 I. Title
 641.6′9′0924   TX747

 ISBN 0-7136-2059-5

Printed in Great Britain by Cedar Colour Ltd.

CONTENTS

INTRODUCTION

I count myself very fortunate to have been born and brought up in a town in the heart of the fenlands around the Wash, with saltings on the seaward and freshwater rivers and lakes landward. My family had little money and so it was necessary for us to have an intimate knowledge of local resources in the way of food, to supplement the family table in the bad times and to add to the family income when things were better.

My father was a great provider. We never went hungry even though, being employed on the local docks before and after the First World War, he was more often out of work than in it. He taught me a lot which will never be forgotten in the many hours I spent with him right up to the time he could no longer get out and about.

Whenever I go back to the Fens I have great fun doing the things described in this book. I have attempted to describe these activities to help those who find themselves for the first time on the saltings, salt marshes and estuaries. It is surprising how many people like the lowly cockle but have no idea where they come from, and the same is true of samphire.

I have gathered samphire from the Wash for over half a century, and propose to deal with it very fully, including a rare recipe for pickling.

SAMPHIRE

SAMPHIRE is a sea-plant (not a seaweed) which grows on saltings anywhere around Britain where conditions are right. I have picked it in Pegwell Bay, Canvey Island, Leigh-on-Sea saltings, North Wales and many other places. You may find it where it has never been picked before because of lack of local knowledge.

The plant starts to show on the mudflats bordering the saltings grass. It also grows in the grass and along the edges of creeks where salt water is tidal. It shows in late May or early June as a little green shoot. From mid-June onwards the plant grows quickly and becomes large enough to pick by the end of July when it is about three or four inches tall, like a beautiful green miniature tree and very fleshy. The best bushy samphire is to be found on the mudflats. The root is firmly emplanted and when pulled out is a clean white and very bushy.

It is most important that before going off in search of samphire you get a sound knowledge of the local tides. Also, unless you have expert knowledge of the area, *never* go on to the salt marshes in a fog. Once the bank is out of sight it is easy to get lost and panic, especially if the creeks are filling. If ever this happens, follow the flow of the tide and you will eventually arrive at the sea-wall or bank.

Once you have found the samphire, grasp the plant by

the thumb and forefingers near the root, and pull. If the earth is wet with rain or the last tide the plant will come out easily, and by holding the root there is less chance of bruising. If the samphire is to be eaten within a day or so, wash off the mud from the roots by swilling or "swidging" the bundles in salt water. Put the bundles on dry land and allow to drain before placing in a canvas bag or clean sack. It will be much lighter to carry this way than samphire with the mud left on, which is sometimes necessary.

If the samphire is to be transported some distance and needs to be kept fresh for a few days, pick it and leave it, as we say "in the mud". Leave the mud on the roots and put it in a small sack. This will be heavy and you will find that walking back over uneven, slippery salt marshes with a load of samphire across your shoulders is for the fit and experienced.

On a good patch the temptation to go on picking is strong and you can easily find yourself with too much to carry back to the sea-wall. Stop picking when you have enough for your immediate use. What you leave will still be there another day.

The season comes to an end by about mid-August. This is when it becomes suitable for pickling and the seeds begin to show. Samphire is self-seeding. Not long ago on a radio programme someone mentioned the great shortage of samphire in 1978. An "expert" went on to say that the people who pick samphire should cut it from the root, implying that it would grow again next year from this root. In fact, samphire goes to seed in late August and then withers if the migrating widgeon doesn't find it first and strip it clean.

The main reason for the shortage of samphire in 1978

was that the seeds were washed out by the high tides and gales of January. They would have been just below the top layer of silt which was washed out, seeds and all. Another recipe for shortage is to pick *all* the samphire leaving none to seed. This can happen where the samphire is very easy to get at.

When the samphire is past its best and getting ready for self-seeding (about the middle and end of August) the plant begins to turn yellow at the base of the fleshy part. A very close examination of the surface will show tiny white particles. These are the seeds. When the tide covers the plant the water washes the seed away and distributes them wherever over the surrounding area. These remain dormant all through the winter. The seeds are covered by the silt deposited by the tides and begin their growth and show a very small green finger about the end of May.

A very common mistake made by samphire pickers is to assume that the samphire is going to seed when it becomes covered with tiny black particles which look like very small seeds. These are not seeds, but baby winkles.

Let us suppose that you have your samphire home and are ready to set about cleaning and preparing for cooking. First, wash the plants under a running tap, and cut off the root just below the base of the plant. Leave a little stem by which to hold it when eating. Wash again under the cold tap, put it in a large saucepan, sprinkle a tablespoon of salt over it, add water to the level of the samphire and bring to the boil. If desired, a pinch of bicarbonate will preserve the green colouring. When the water boils reduce the heat and remove the scum from the top (no matter how well you wash the samphire this scum always appears). Simmer for 15 to 20 minutes. To test whether it is ready, take a piece and pull the green flesh from the inner stalk. If it comes away cleanly the samphire is cooked. Empty the contents of the pan into a colander and pour boiling water over the samphire.

There is no one right way to eat samphire but our family way was as follows: The table would be laid with large plates, salt, pepper and vinegar, and brown bread and butter. The colander was placed in the centre of the table on a large plate to catch the draining water. The procedure was then to put salt, pepper and vinegar on one's plate and lift a few plants on to it. Holding a piece by the stem it was dipped into the vinegar, salt and pepper and pulled sideways through the teeth to remove the green flesh from the stem which is then discarded.

There are, of course, many other ways of serving samphire. I once introduced samphire to a French lady who had a flair for cooking. She came up with a plate of hot shredded samphire tossed in hot butter and topped

Robinson's Bookshop

THE LANES,
BRIGHTON.
Telephone:
Brighton 29012

with poached eggs. With brown bread and butter this was a very light, tasty and satisfying dish.

If you prefer to buy your samphire from a market stall you should allow about a pound per person as a starter to find out if they like it. There are people who do not care for it, but they are very few and far between.

I am often asked to describe the taste of samphire and the nearest I can get is to liken it to long French beans, or string beans as my mother called them, sliced lengthwise, boiled and garnished with vinegar, salt and pepper.

Another aspect of samphire cookery which extremely few people know of, is the pickling process. I am indebted to my sister and brother-in-law for this – he was a professional picker for fifty years. He gathered six or eight large bags a day, and carried them to the sea-wall about a mile away – no mean feat. They have jars of pickled samphire over five years old in perfect condition. Pickled samphire should be eaten sparingly as a side dish, for flavour only. It will last for ages if properly closed and stored when not in use. Here is the recipe:

PICKLED SAMPHIRE

The samphire for pickling should be collected near the end of the season, about mid- to end-August. It is then large and bushy, about six inches high, all green except the base of the plant which is beginning to turn yellow.

For normal cooking and eating as previously described, this end-of-season samphire is "woody" and needs a longer cooking time. It is also "going to seed".

When collecting and transporting make sure the samphire is not bruised. Wash well under cold running tap water, discard any damaged plants and cut off the

13

root close to the base of the plant, leaving just enough to hold the stem. Put up some "washing lines" of string, preferably under cover, and peg out the plants to dry. This will probably take two or three days.

You will need a large earthenware jar with a wide, open neck and a tight-fitting cork for sealing when the samphire is "done". Place the dry samphire in the *DRY* jar between layers of pickling spice. When the jar is almost full but not pressed down, fill the jar to the top with vinegar to cover the samphire.

Place in an oven and bring to the boil, then simmer gently for four hours, topping up with vinegar as the level gets lower. At the end of this operation try a piece for easy shredding from the stalk. If the flesh comes off easily the pickling is done. After four hours, turn off the heat and leave in the oven for twelve hours to cool very slowly.

Remove from the oven, cover the neck with a clean cloth and leave to cool. When cold, press the cork home securely and store the jar in a dry cool place.

When needed for use take two or three plants from the jar and shred the flesh on to a plate. It is delicious with cold dishes treated as a garnish and not eaten in large quantities. It is also very good with lowly bread and cheese.

If one were fortunate enough to be invited to Christmas dinner in any house in the fishermen's quarter of Lynn, there would most likely be a bit of pickled samphire on the menu somewhere. There was always a jar of pickled samphire on the floor of our pantry.

AFTERTHOUGHTS

Gathering samphire can be heavy work but I remember some ways in which it used to be made easier. When I was a boy one professional samphire-picker had a pony and trap. I have seen that pony and trap way out on the mudflats with the tide lapping the wheels but Old Billy knew the way back to the bank without crossing a gully. It was an easy ride all the way home.

My dad used to go out by boat when the tide was flowing out in the river and arrive on the top of the salting and mudflats before the tide left them dry. We would then spend the whole day in sunshine or rain filling bag after bag with samphire "in the mud". These were loaded aboard and we would come in with the tide. During the days and years of unemployment between the wars this was a vital part of his income. The samphire was sold from door to door, washed and clean, at three pence for a large bowlful. Any surplus went to the local fish shop.

Another means of transport from the marsh to the sea-wall was the one we often employed when there was no boat or pony and trap available. Where the salt grass and vegetation covered the mud for a long distance from the sea-wall to the mudflats, where the best bushy samphire grew, we looked for a creek leading to the sea-wall. Bags were filled and put in the creek to await the tide. They then floated in to the sea-wall where we lifted them out of the water and left them to drain.

I have also used a gun-punt which was floated out to the samphire grounds and left in a nearby creek. The bags were loaded crossways and floated back to the sea-wall or sea-bank.

Samphire has other names. One dictionary describes it

15

as a form of sea fennel, and it is known in France as St Peter's herb. In Essex I have heard it called sea spinach. Around the Wash, one of the best places in the British Isles for samphire in my opinion, it is called samphire or sanfa, and has been referred to as "the wildfowler's succulent dish". I have myself often enjoyed chewing it raw when out on the marshes searching for wildfowl.

BUTT DRAGGING AND JOBBING

"**B**UTT" is the term used on the Norfolk coast on the south side of the Wash for the flounder. I knew them only as butts until I moved away from the area. We caught them with rod and line using uncooked shrimps as bait, in the river and in the Fisher Fleet where the boats unloaded their shrimp catches.

Here I will describe and illustrate a method of catching them peculiar to the River Ouse outlet area. It entails the use of a "drag" which is hauled along the river bottom by a boat moving with the tide, or by hand in shallow water where one can wade with the drag about ten feet behind. With this implement you can catch as many butts as you can carry back. Even though hooked, the small ones will survive if taken off the hook carefully and put back. If you can feel the shrimps between your toes as you walk through the shallows you can be sure that butts will be around. They are just under the surface of the sandy mud with only eyes and mouth showing ready to pick off the shrimps. If the water is too clear the butts will spot the drag coming and get out of the way, shooting away in a flurry of sand and mud. One would do better in these conditions to use a net method. But when there is a slight breeze which stirs up the bottom and makes the water murky, one can walk in calf-deep water and actually stand on the flat-fish.

To make a drag for hand-hauling you will need a flat bar of mild steel about five feet long, two inches wide, and about three-eighths of an inch thick. Starting half an inch in from the end and half an inch from the edge, drill quarter-inch holes along the length of the bar about three inches apart. Cut off the end of the bar half an inch from the last hole.

Drill a hole about a foot from each end half an inch in from the edge and equidistant between the existing holes. These two holes are attachment points for the hauling traces.

The next step is to make this bar into a rake-like instrument using cod hooks and gutter bolts. Cod hooks usually have the eye turned at right-angles to the bend and barb and will be about three inches long with an inch-and-a-half bend. Gutter bolts are short and smooth headed.

Each hook is placed *under* the bar, projecting forward and the gutter bolt inserted through the eye of the hook and then through a hole in the bar. The washer and the nut are then threaded on and well-tightened, making sure that the hook underneath is at a right-angle to the bar. When all the hooks are attached you have a fearsome weapon indeed and one that should be treated with respect.

Attach the wire traces to the bar by means of screw shackles with quarter-inch bolts at the points on the bar where the trace holes have previously been drilled. The traces are brought together and attached to a towing line of half-inch nylon, about ten feet long.

You are now equipped with a tool with which to go

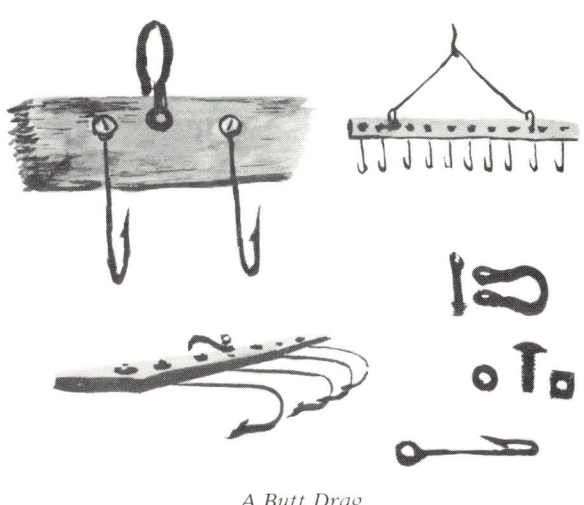

A Butt Drag

dragging for butts. As you haul the drag along behind you will feel the hooks dragging through the sandy silt. When a fish becomes impaled the drag will swim. If you are fishing near the edge drag it ashore, take the fish off the hook and place in the side-bag. Put the small ones back. If you want to remove the fish while standing in the water, lift the drag with the hooks away from you. Hold the drag with one hand and with the other grasp the fish across the backbone where it is firm or with a thumb inside a gill and detach it from the hook. Drop the drag back into the water very carefully with the hooks away from you. A cockle impaled on one hook will make the drag swim and must be cleared before the drag will fish properly. One memorable day with my daughter, then aged about seven, we caught so many fish that it was an effort to carry them the three miles across the mudflats. The drag was catching as many as four at a time from water which was alive with shrimps. The largest was a three-pounder.

A drag will pick up all kinds of flatfish from the bottom. I have caught soles, plaice, brill, sandlings, and once a nice thornback near the East Side Beacon.

Drag sizes can be adjusted according to your strength – I have found a five-footer ideal, but then I was a six-footer and twelve-and-a-half stone. But the pattern and the distance between the hooks remain the same. The fish not worth catching slip between the hooks as they would through the mesh of a net.

If you are using the butt-drag from a boat it can be a six-footer, but the trace and shackles should be heavier and the line to the boat heavier. A 12-foot rowing boat is ideal in a fast-flowing river. The idea is to straddle the tide and lower the drag to the bottom. The deeper it goes the more weight is needed which can be obtained by attaching lead bars to the top of the drag. We used to work two five-footers, one fore and one aft. Whilst one was being hauled the other line was moved to midships to keep the boat broadside to the tide.

Do remember that on any river there can be snags on the bottom. To prevent accidents, do not tie your drag-lines inboard, unless you have allowed plenty of slack. When the drag touches bottom let it go and hold as it starts fishing and you feel the hooks pulling through the sand and mud. Put a marlin pin in the rowlock hole on the top rail and take two turns of the drag-line around it. If the drag snags pull out the marlin pin and let the long line pay out, you can then pull the other drag inboard. You should then row upriver against the tide beyond the point where the drag snagged and it will usually free itself.

I used to go out with the tide, dragging all the way, to the middle of the Wash, then go ashore to fill a couple of bags with cockles and finally return to the middle and come back in with the tide, dragging all the way. It was a full day usually starting about four or five o'clock in the morning. But it was good fun with something to show for my trouble.

THE BUTT PICK OR JOBBER

An alternative tool using the same principle is the butt pick. This was used in deep-water gulleys where boat handling was difficult or where the bottom was too soft to support a surface drag.

Basically it was a rake, the business end comprising a straight hardwood bar through which barbed spikes were threaded and bolted on. It required some skill in metalwork, since the barbed spikes had to be handmade, threaded and the ends filed into a barb-shape.

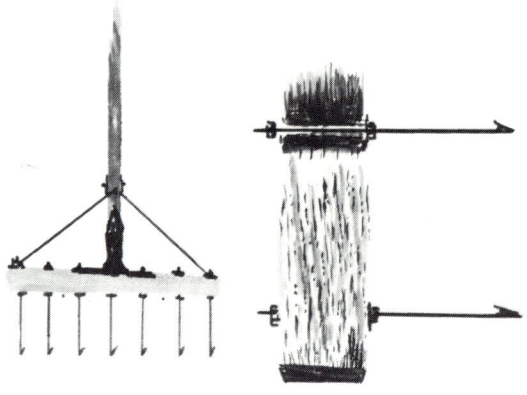

A Butt Jobber

EELS

T HESE delicious fish can be found in all manner of
waterways, drains, fresh water dykes, lakes, ponds
and rivers; they are equally at home in saltwater rivers,
creeks and estuaries; wherever there is water, the eel can
be found. They can be caught in many ingenious ways
devised to suit local conditions. In the Fens, there being
no shortage of water there were, and are plenty of eels.
Here are some of the methods used when my dad was a
boy, which he showed me, and which are the same today,
with little alteration except in the use of modern materials
which have taken the place of the old-fashioned hand-
woven willow traps and baskets used in trapping.

Everyone who goes fishing knows of the hook, line and
sinker method. An eel on a hook is a messy affair, and it is
best to cut the line near the eel's mouth, bang the eel on
the head and drop it into the bag. The hook can be
recovered when the eel is cleaned and gutted.

The method used mostly in the Fens is "babbing". It is
simple and clean, uses no hooks, and so does not injure or
harm the small eels, which can be put into a land-locked
lake or pond and allowed to grow for food in the future.

The materials needed are simple and cost little or
nothing: a stout cane about six feet long for boat use, or
nine feet for use on land; a strong line of nylon/cotton as

used in net-making and about fifteen feet in length; a small assortment of lead weights of four, eight, twelve ounces; some strong wool/worsted; a needle about nine inches long which can be made from one-sixteenth round steel flattened at one end through which the eye is drilled (we improvised by using the stays from an old umbrella). Large, juicy earth-worms are needed, the big blackheads (about nine to twelve inches long and very fat) that come up at night. I called these "night-gobblers" and used to collect mine after a rain, in the dark using a small torch. They can be bought from bait shops nowadays. About fifty would make up two or three nice babs. Use one bab at a time, keeping the other two in reserve. When eels are on the feed they will tear the babs to pieces.

Thread the needle with about three feet of double wool, knotted at the ends. Put the sharpened end of the needle into the mouth of the worm and thread the length of the worm along the needle and pass down to the end of the thread. Keep the worm straight, not bunched. Follow on with other worms until the full length of wool is used up. Cut from the needle and tie to the other knotted end. Wind this large loop of worms around spread fingers to make small loops about three or four inches in diameter. Tie these small loops together at any point and then secure to the main line. This line should be tied securely to the end of the rod and wound round it according to the depth you will be fishing. In strong running water, a heavier weight is needed to get and hold the bait straight down.

Sit comfortably at one end of the boat, which ought to be anchored or moored in some other way. Lower the bab over the side until it touches bottom, then lift off the bottom slightly. The pole should be a shade up from horizontal. The whole thing will balance in such a way that anything touching the bab will be felt. In salt water lift a bit higher to keep clear of crabs. An eel will attack the bab like a small shark. When you feel him tugging lift in one swift movement (no snatching) clear of the water and swing into the boat. Shake the eel(s) from the bab and carry on fishing.

When the eel grabs at the worms, the curved teeth of the eel catch in the worsted and it can be hauled out alive, unharmed and clean. A small-mesh net stretched loosely across the boat will hold the eels and save cleaning the eel slime from the boat.

Another method of making a bab without threading worms on to worsted is as follows: Half a pound or so of worms (offal or the like) can be placed inside the foot of a nylon stocking. The weight can be fixed to the top where it joins the main line. The eels grab at the filled stocking and get their teeth caught in the mesh long enough for you to haul them out.

The best time to bab for eels is during the summer, when they are swimming (they go to earth during the winter and hibernate). Choose a moonless night with plenty of cloud, no wind and a very "close" or humid atmosphere. These are the ideal conditions but the method works in daylight also.

When fishing a river or pond from the bank, a nine- or twelve-foot bamboo pole should be used. Cast out several feet and when you feel the eel take the bab. Haul out smoothly (again no snatching) over the head to the bank behind you. Scoop up the eel before it gets back to the water and put in a keep-net to keep fresh.

TRAPS

"Eel-baskets" and "Grigs" are a common sight in any out-house around the Fens. Eel-baskets are made from wicker-weave or wood-and-willow, and are generally about three feet long, and about nine inches across. One end is in the form of a lid and the other end is an inverted funnel tapering to an inch and a half across. The usual bait is stinking meat, fish-heads or offal. A similar trap can be made from nylon or plastic-covered wire mesh moulded to the shape of the traditional basket around a wooden framework. Don't forget to put a lead weight at each end to hold bottom.

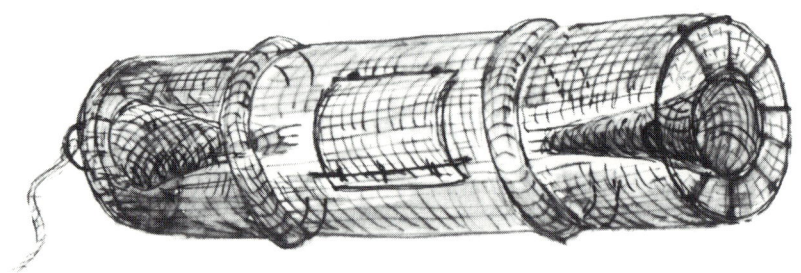

An Eel Basket

To make a grig, begin by obtaining a piece of hardwood for the base, three feet by one foot and one and a half inches thick. Use strip-metal for the supports as indicated in the drawing and cover with chicken wire, shrimp netting or whatever. Next, at each end fashion inward-facing funnels from pieces of mesh tapering to about one and a half inches, and a hinged lid for the top. This lid is not only for extracting the catch but also to attach the bait which might otherwise be washed out of the cage. The grig should be weighted to hold bottom and well-secured to the recovery line.

One grig like this will keep a man well supplied with eels and several can make it a profitable sideline.

An Eel Grig

SIMPLER METHODS

As a boy I used a primitive sort of trap very successfully. I took a sack, put some straw, bait and weights in it and tied the neck around a piece of drainpipe. The eels would enter by way of the pipe, eat the food and then curl up in the straw to sleep it off. I would leave this trap in one place for a few days before recovering it and seldom found an empty sack. You might even dispense with the sack and push the straw and bait into the drainpipe itself. Eels seem to love a dark hole in which to lie up.

WINTER EELING WITH PILGAR OR GLAVE

Eels hibernate during the winter, burrowing into the mud up to a foot deep or at the bottom of the bank. Then the Fensmen would spear them with a pilgar or glave on the end of a fifteen-foot pole.

They usually operated from a flat-bottomed punt, but also worked from the bank of a stream and in shallow water. The body of the pilgar is shaped like a three-pronged fork, the ends being so formed as to guide the eel up between the slots, which hold the eel securely enough to haul it up and out. When properly made, this tool, like the glave, will last for years with care and can easily be made by your local blacksmith or any handyman. All edges should be rounded and smooth, to avoid cutting the body of the eel.

A variation of design is shown in the drawing which indicates how two needles may be attached to the head of the pilgar.

The glave, like the pilgar, is the size of a garden spade. As the drawing shows, this tool has no needles or narrow tines to bend or break. The cutaway part, where the eel is

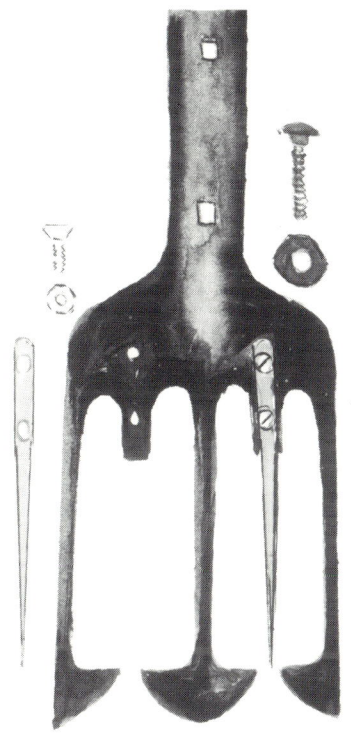

A Pilgar

A Glave

29

held when struck, need only be about three-sixteenths of an inch wide. Any eels which can wriggle out of that width won't be worth catching anyway. Like the pilgar, this tool can be made lighter by having only one zig-zag cut-out.

To remove an eel from the glave, prise the blades apart in opposite directions and let the eel fall out. If made from suitable steel, the glave blades will spring back into their original position.

These tools were devised for fishing in fresh water, but can be employed in salt water if eels have become trapped there. This often happens when a sea-wall has been laid across saltings to enclose land, as often happens around the Wash.

Another little-known method of taking eels requires the use of a small rowing boat during the summer months when eels are swimming. It is only effective in tidal saltwater tributaries.

Collect and bundle together lengths of straight willow or other straight, thin branches. The bundle should be about three feet long and about one foot in diameter. One person should be able to manage six of these bundles. At the top of the tide and upstream as far as one cares to go, drop the bundles overboard, one by one, at intervals of a few yards. When the tide begins to ebb the bundles will slowly float along with the tide out to sea. During this journey swimming eels should come up and wriggle into the bundles almost as if they wanted a free ride. When near the river outlet, with the aid of a boat-hook swiftly scoop the bundles up and into the boat.

PREPARATION AND COOKING

The first decision to be made is whether or not to skin the eel. If you want to make "jelled" eels the skin is left on.

To clean eels use a sharp, pointed knife with a three- or four-inch blade. Slit the belly from below the vent to beneath the jaws. Pull out the guts and cut off the head if the skin is to be left on. If not, cut through the backbone behind the head, without breaking the skin, bend the head back and pull the head and skin back to the tail in a smooth, peeling action.

Wash the cleaned eels in running water, and leave to soak in a bowl of water to which has been added a large spoonful of salt and an eggcup of vinegar. This both cleans the fish and makes it white.

I like my eels boiled with thyme. Cut the fish into two-inch chunks, bring to the boil and simmer till tender. Save the liquid which can be thickened to make a sauce. If you like "jelled" eels, pour the eels and liquor into a dish (or dishes), allow to cool and place in the fridge where the "mess" (as we say in Norfolk) will set.

You can also fry the chunks of eel, either rolled in flour and shallow-fried or dipped in batter and deep-fried.

CRAB-CLAYING

I OFTEN used to go out on the shrimping boats when I was a boy. When the nets were emptied on to the decks there were always, in addition to the shrimps, a number of small crabs, about two or three inches long. Because they were so small and inconvenient to prepare they were, and are, wrongly classed as inedible. The clays, by the way, were the local name for the two main claws.

On these trips I used to keep the clays and would often have enough to fill three saucepans by the end of the day. After washing, they were boiled (turning that beautiful red colour), allowed to cool and eaten by the family.

There were other ways of getting a supply of crab clays. Our favourite method was to catch them with a "bab" as described in the chapter on eels. When worms for the bab were hard to come by we used to beg fish offal from our local fishmonger. These were put into a bag made from lace curtains, weighted and lowered to the sea or river bottom from boat, bridge or sea-wall.

As I grew older and more expert, I devised a crab-trap. This was baited and lowered into tidal saltwater streams, creeks and gullies. The small crabs we caught were to provide bait for the saltwater traps in the main river but we kept the claws for the table.

A simple trap to catch crabs may be made as follows: Gather some willow branches and soak well in water until they are very pliable. Take two of the stouter branches and make two hoops – one two feet in diameter, the other about five inches in diameter. Using the large hoop as a base, join the two with lengths of willow to make a shape like a half-sphere. Fill the circular base-shape with close basket-weave and the sides with open-weave so that the crabs can see the bait inside.

A Crab Trap

You will have to place weights in it if you are using it in tidal waters and the recovery lines should be attached as shown in the drawing to avoid tipping the basket when lifting. The baskets can be left submerged for two or three days, or, if used in places that are uncovered at low water, they should be staked and checked at the next low water.

The fruit of your labours should be washed well in running water. Place in a large saucepan, cover with water and add a spoonful of cooking salt. When they come to the boil, take off the heat immediately and empty into a colander to drain, and then wash again under running water. They will now have turned a beautiful shade of red. When cold the shells can be cracked between the thumb and forefinger.

Another and even more simple device is the hoop and catch net.

Take an old bicycle wheel, remove the spokes and hub, and attach a net bag to the rim. Attach the whole thing to a rod and line by means of four lines attached at equal intervals around the wheel.

Attach the bait (fish heads, etc.) to where the four strings join the main line. Drop the wheel and net over the side of a boat to the bottom of any saltwater creek or inlet and leave for a while. After a while lift strongly. Whatever is at the bait will fall into the net suspended beneath. You should find some crabs, from which the clays can be taken, and sometimes by the way of a bonus, a nice eel drops into the net. I have used this method on one side of the boat while saltwater angling on the other side.

CRABS

T H E large crabs we see on sale in the fishmonger's shop can be found all round Britain and Ireland. The crab-trap described in the chapter on crab-claying can also be used for catching large crabs.

All the best places around our shores are regularly fished by the local fishermen, but there are still some spots to be found where a trap or "pot" can be placed to yield a few nice crabs. My own method entails the use of a piece of wood with a metal hook attached to the end. Choose a spot on the seashore where the sand is flat at very low water and with rock formations, a typical example being Old Hunstanton and Holme-next-the-Sea.

A knowledge of the local tides is vital. The highest tide also means the lowest low water, exposing and uncovering rock formations which are usually concealed even at ordinary low water. The highest and lowest tides occur twice a month, but a local tide-table is always your best bet. When the time of the lowest tide has been determined, walk out with the retreating tide, armed with a strong bag and the hook. The rocks at the water's edge will be uncovered and there you will find the crabs hiding. Push the hook into the holes and crevices. If a crab is at home it will grab the intruder with both claws with such ferocity that it may be withdrawn from its hiding place. Usually you can shake the crabs into your sack; if it drops to the sand it will immediately hold both claws in the "on guard" position and make for the nearest rock. Put the hook between its claws and it will probably grab the hook again, giving you another chance.

Anything under four inches should be left to grow bigger. Never take more than you need, they will still be there next time the rocks are uncovered.

Do not catch crabs when they are off-season – from about mid-October to late May. During this time they shed their shell and hide away until the shell hardens.

Crabs should be kept alive until wanted for cooking. If you live by the sea they can be kept fresh and alive in a large wooden box about a foot deep, three feet long and two feet wide. Drill holes all over the box, weight it, put the crabs inside and keep it submerged in saltwater. Otherwise, keep the crabs in a thick wet sack in a cool place.

Very few people know the correct way to cook them. Before the crabs are needed for cooking, place in lukewarm fresh water, leave them for several hours. This acts as a soporific and enables you to handle them without any fear of getting nipped. Next, scrub the crabs with salt on a stiff brush. Then prepare a large boiler containing enough water to cover the crabs to be cooked. For every crab add a tablespoonful of salt. Put the crabs into the cold water and bring to the boil for fifteen or twenty minutes by which time they will have changed colour to the familiar red of the cooked crab. Remove from the water and allow to cool.

To open the cooked crab, hold the top shell in the left hand and the claws and legs in the right, and exert pressure until they part. Inside will be seen the "dead men" – greyish-green pieces in the centre of the body. *Remove these pieces.* If you are not sure, ask your local fishmonger for advice. All the rest of the crab meat can be eaten. *Never* put live crabs in boiling water. Apart from possible cruelty, the legs will break off and the body will fill with water. An alternative method of killing crabs before cooking is as follows: turn the crab onto its back, open the flap in the centre of the lower half and push a knitting needle straight into the vent, right through to the inside of the top shell. This kills the crab immediately. It can then be scrubbed clean and cooked in the normal manner.

Incidentally, if you are lucky enough to bag a reasonably-sized lobster it can be dropped into the boiling water in which the crabs are cooking, and given about twenty minutes. As it goes into the boiling water a small shriek may be heard. This is *not* the lobster shrieking on contact with the boiling water as I have heard said – it is the shell of the lobster contracting very suddenly in the sudden heat. When cooked, allow to cool and then cut through the shell from head to tail. Remove the long thin tube running from the stomach to beneath the tail. This is the straight gut of the lobster; it can be poisonous or, at least, very unpalatable, and should be removed. Incidentally, a live lobster put into boiling water will rise to the top when cooked.

SHRIMPS

I HAVE never thought much of the traditional shrimp-net to be seen hanging outside seaside shops. Instead, here is a more efficient design, and portable. Obtain a five-foot square of small-mesh netting. Fold it once to make a triangle and sew up the two shorter sides. Then cut along the long edge to form a triangular bag. Tie a length of thin steel bar to one of the cut edges and a row of corks to the other. A towing line and triangular trace should be attached to each lower corner of the metal frame. The lower lip of the mouth is tied to the frame.

You are now ready to begin trawling. Wade in to knee or thigh depth and place the net, metal-bar side down, on the sea-bottom. Trawl the gear along about eight feet behind you and you should find that the shrimps will be

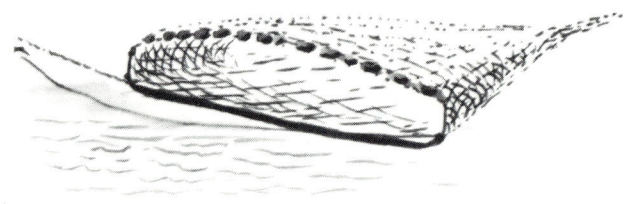

A Drag Shrimp Net

disturbed by the bar bumping along over the sand and will leap up to be caught in the net which is kept open by the corks. After a while, take the net ashore and check your catch. Keep any shrimps in a bucket of seawater.

To cook, wash well and place in a large saucepan. Cover with water, add salt, and bring to the boil. This should be enough cooking time and the shrimps should have turned from grey-green to brown in colour.

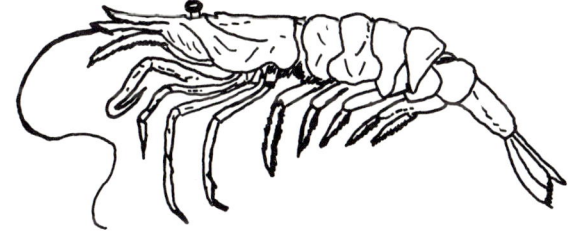

CLAMS

C LAMS have often been called "the poor man's oyster", and looked upon as a poor relation, probably because of their appearance when in the shell, their size, and the fact that they need to be cleaned properly before eating.

You will find clams in creeks and drainways having more sand than mud. Look for clean, round holes in the surface of the sandy mud. The clam will be about a foot down, standing on end. The feeding trunk comes from between the two shells and, when stretched, may be over a foot long.

Dig down until the shell is found, and finish the digging with your fingers so as not to damage the shell.

After washing and scrubbing, open the shell with a sharp, pointed knife inserted at the hinge to cut the muscle. Clean away the flanges around the inside of the shell. The trunk, which is a tough concertina-shaped muscle, can be removed by holding with the thumb and forefinger and cutting at the base where it joins the stomach of the fish.

Some people like to scald the clams before eating, but otherwise wash well in running water and garnish with vinegar (or lemon juice), salt and pepper. A dry or medium white wine goes well with clams, as does a pint of real ale.

The very large blue-clams are not very popular as they come from smelly mud. They are usually very large and are none too palatable. It is still possible to get small chalk clams, particularly on the North Norfolk coast. These are young, tender and very tasty. They are about three inches long and have a white shell. The best place to find them is at the base of the beach where the shingle gives way to sandy mud. In this area the clam is usually down about nine inches. Lift pieces of green seaweed carefully and now and again you will see the clam trunk disappearing down the small round hole beneath. The hole down to the clam can be followed easily by digging down to one side of it. When the clam is uncovered treat it gently so as not to damage it. Clean and prepare as previously described.

WHELKS

T HE whelk is another sea-snail found all round our shores. The whelk fisherman will fish with pots in a very professional manner and in the most prolific areas. But while sea angling in places where whelks are not normally harvested, I have often hauled up whelks attracted by the expensive and succulent lug-worm on the hook.

Cook as for winkles, adding about a tablespoon of salt to a quart of water. Bring to the boil and leave for five or ten minutes. They are fully cooked when they can be removed easily from the shell with a narrow fork. Empty into a colander to drain and cool. When cool, take them out of their shells and remove the horny cap or lid. Now a word of warning – on the rounded and thickest part of the whelk and just under the surface can be found the "worm" or stomach. When one is expert it is easy to place this part between the front teeth and bite it out clean. Otherwise, extract it with a fork and throw it away. Even if you get cooked whelks from a stall you should bite out the "worm".

AFTERTHOUGHT

If one is lucky enough to live near a rocky coast which is not being fished by the whelkers, a whelk-pot or crab-trap baited with anything fishy can be lowered to the bottom and retrieved some hours later with enough whelks to make a nice meal. Throw the small ones back to grow and catch later.

WINKLES

WINKLES are tasty little sea-snails. They are black in colour and anything up to an inch and a half across when fully grown. They are common all round the British Isles and across the Channel. At low water, search for them in pools among the rocks and on the shingle at the base of the beach. Leave the small ones, picking only those about an inch across or larger. Those clinging to rocks are alive and the live ones on the move will leave a trail like a snail. If in doubt, leave them.

Wash the winkles well and cover with cold water in a saucepan. For every pint (measure in an ordinary beer mug) add a spoonful of salt. Bring to the boil and simmer for five minutes. Take one out, cool, remove the black cap. Insert a pin into the opening and extract the winkle. If it leaves the shell easily the winkles are done and can be removed from the water, drained and allowed to cool.

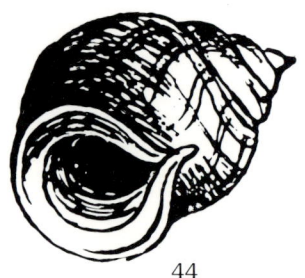

MUSSELS

M USSELS flourish all round Great Britain wherever saltwater ebbs and flows over the shore. Most mussel beds are "laid" by the local fishermen, the young mussels being left to grow to an agreed size before being harvested. Only those over two inches long may be taken. The season for collecting mussels covers all the months with an "R" in them, i.e. September to April.

These mussel beds should be left severely alone but there are many places in which "wild" mussels can be found, look for clean ones (without barnacles), collect in season, wash well, and separate.

Place a quantity in a large pot, cover with cold water and add one teaspoonful of salt per quart of mussels. Bring to the boil. As soon as the mussels open, empty into a colander and drain. The meat of the mussel should be a rich creamy yellow and should almost fill the shell. When cool, remove the mussel from the shell. It is necessary to pull out the piece of weed attached to the "tongue" in the centre. Wash all the cooked mussels in clean running water and strain off excess water.

Mussels are usually served simply, with lemon juice or vinegar and brown bread and butter. I prefer mine hot, straight from the shell, and then dipped in vinegar. They can also be boiled first then sautéd.

Mussel

COCKLES

COCKLES thrive in the sandy shores all around our coast. An outstanding area is the Wash, with its acres of sands and mudflats. Local fishermen have made the catching of cockles and mussels into a well-established industry. Other good places are the Thames estuary from Leigh-on-Sea, off Shoeburyness, and the mouth of the Crouch, on both north and south banks. There are many others too.

The cockle lies about two inches beneath the surface of the sandy mud. Look for small holes in the surface sometimes with a small piece of green seaweed attached – there is usually a cockle beneath. When they are plentiful you can hear them "singing".

The cockle is a round, white fluted shell which opens on a hinge. Cockles about an inch across are the best, tender and sweetest. Wash them well to rid the shells of sand and mud. Put in a saucepan and just cover with water, adding a spoonful of salt. When the shells begin to open, empty the lot into a colander and wash through with plenty of hot water.

Have ready on the table, brown bread and butter and medium-sized plates containing salt, pepper and vinegar. Empty the cockles from the shell into the salt, pepper and vinegar on the plate and eat them with your fingers. If you like them cold, remove the cockles from the shells and put in a container in the fridge.

Cockle

NOTES ON SHELL FISH

I HAVE always had great sympathy for people who are allergic to shell fish and are, therefore, unable to enjoy this delicious food. But even if you have never suffered any ill-effects from eating shell fish, there are a few points you must bear in mind when collecting them.

Never collect whelks, mussels, cockles, winkles or clams which are loose on top of the sand. Clams and cockles live *in* the sand and you cannot be sure that they are alive and fresh unless they are dug out of the sand. Winkles move around the rocks and sand. They are either firmly attached to rocks or on the move leaving behind them a trail like a garden snail. Never take one or any rolling around loose.

Mussels should be over two inches long, with closed shells, and linked to others by the seaweed on which they feed. They should also come from a clean sea in tidal water. Collect only when there's an "R" in the month. This applies also to whelks, clams, winkles, cockles and clams.

Always wash well before and after cooking and eat as soon after cooking as possible. Do not store in the refrigerator for more than a few days.

When washing mussels before cooking look for any with open shells and throw them out. One mussel that has gone off can spoil all the rest in the cooking.

NET-BRAIDING

IN THIS age of buying everything off-the-shelf, the art and knowledge of net-braiding is gradually being lost. Ready-made nets in all sizes are available in almost every fishing tackle shop. They are usually made of stiff nylon and do not last very long. Once the knots and methods have been learned you can forget about machine-made net and make your own for all occasions and in all weights and mesh sizes.

Net needles (or shuttles) can be obtained at most ship chandlers who cater for the needs of professional fishermen. They come in all sizes of length and width – small and narrow for the small mesh and larger and wider for the heavier nets. A set of plastic needles does not cost very much. A range of sizes from half an inch to an inch and a half wide will meet all your needs.

The next item required is the "shale", or mesh-gauge. This is a six-inch strip of flat, smooth hardwood, about an eighth of an inch thick and very slightly tapered. The width of the shale determines the size of the mesh – the wider the shale, the bigger the mesh. Before the advent of plastic the needles and shales were made from whale-bone, and these are now very hard to come by.

The net-making cotton can be obtained from the chandler in various weights on spools. The old pure cotton has now been replaced by the far superior non-shrinking, nylon cotton which is very strong and pliable.

To fill the needle, loop the line on the centre pin, take the line round the end of the needle to the centre spike on the other side, around it and back round the end, round the centre spike, and so on, back and forth, until the needle is holding a fat length of the line. Remember to char the ends of cut nylon to stop it unravelling.

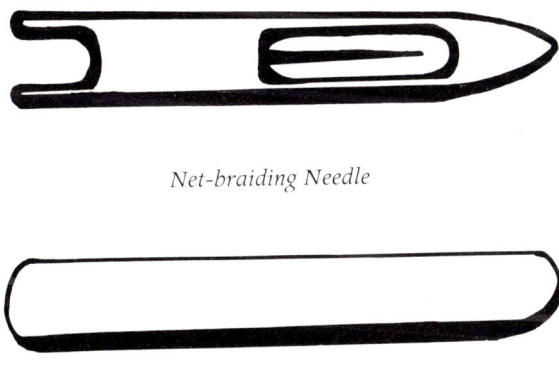

Net-braiding Needle

Shale

Next tie a loop of line around a secure hook on a wall or post, then tie the end of the line from the needle to the loop. Take a turn round the shale and make the knot shown in the illustration. Remove the shale from the loop made. Feed the line on the needle round the shale, knot, feed it through the same loop, around the shale, and tie again. This has made two loops. Take out the shale and start another row, increasing by doing an extra loop at the

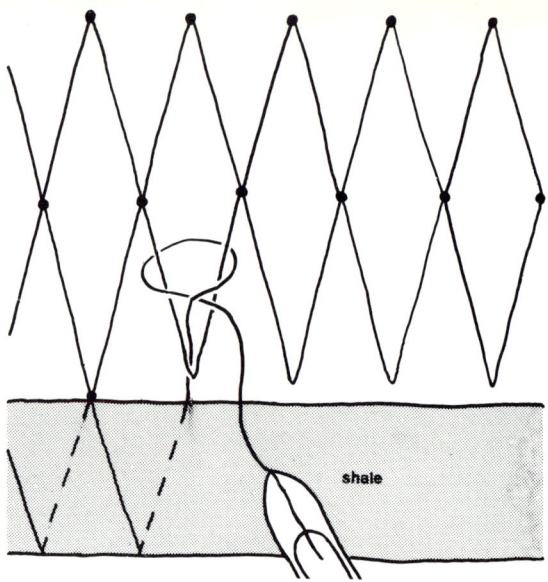

Making a Knot

end. By increasing at the end of every row the net will increase in width. You can, of course, decrease or enlarge the size of the net by changing to smaller or larger shales as the net progresses. When you can tie the knot correctly and keep a uniform tension other shapes and sizes can be worked with a bit of ingenuity.

You may find it easier to begin by taking a small piece of ready-made net and using our method to extend it. This is known as a "swidge", a common term among East Anglian fishermen who made their own nets.

You can make nets for all kinds of jobs – from purse-nets for ferreting, to large nets to cover the width of a tidal creek (useful for catching mullet in the summer). From the days when fishermen's wives and mothers made nets (long since gone) I remember attractive neck-scarves made from two blending colours of three-ply wool in small mesh.

A BOOT-JACK

M ANY of the activities described in previous chapters can only be done whilst wearing rubber boots whether knee-length or thigh-length.

Providing they are dry inside, nothing more than a little talcum powder to lubricate the inside of the boot and the outer sock will be necessary to get them on.

Getting them off is not always so simple. It is a well-known fact that even after only a short period of use the inside of the boot becomes very damp. Without a boot-jack the usual method is for the wearer to sit with outstretched leg whilst the "puller-off" takes a firm grip on the (often very dirty) boot. The rest is brute force – the boot comes away eventually, but what a perform-ance.

The boot-jack does the job cleanly and neatly and is also suitable for riding boots, rubber boots, ladies' sheepskin and long leather boots. Anyone can make a boot-jack from two pieces of hardwood.

Obtain a piece of flat hardwood (oak, ash, beech) about 10 inches long, 5 inches wide and one inch thick. Cut into one end a rounded "U" shape to about four inches deep and just less than the width of the heel where the heel fits into the boot.

Round all the corners with a rasp and glasspaper. You

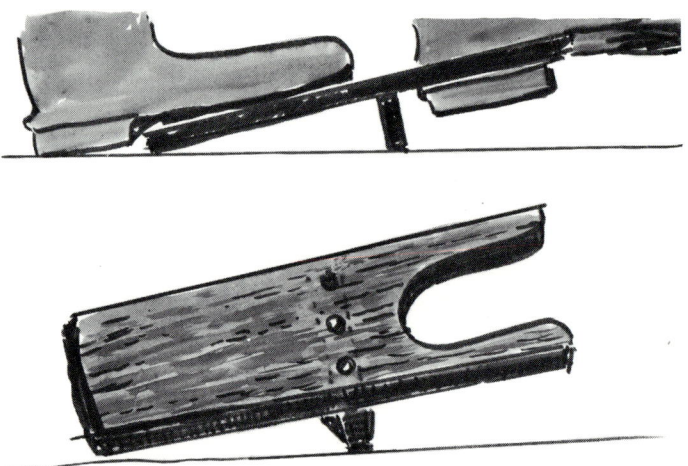

can glue a rubber strip inside the U part but providing the heel of the boot fits properly into jack, the added rubber strip is not really necessary.

The next piece of wood goes across the bottom of the jack about an inch or so behind the U part. This should be about one-and-a-half inches wide and about one-inch thick.

Drill three screw-holes equi-distant across the top of the jack to attach the strip of wood underneath.

When finished and placed on the floor, the U part of the jack should be raised at the right height to receive the heel of the boot. The other foot should be placed on the jack where it touches the ground to hold it firmly. The foot comes out of the boot with ease, even out of thigh-boots.

In country cottages around the Fens the boot-jack was in everyday use hanging in the out-house along with the mole-traps, snares and nets, etc.

Three sizes (small, medium and large) will cope with the needs of the family or you can make a double jack with a large U at one end and a smaller U at the other.

Many years ago, at a farmhouse in Norfolk, I saw a very nice version of the boot-jack. It had obviously been made by a very accomplished blacksmith who fully understood what he was making. The main raised platform was flat one-inch steel, about 24 inches long and about 10 inches wide. It was set on legs to give the platform an upward tilt to where the boot heels were placed and two uprights in loop form were attached each end to act as hand-holds. It also incorporated four different-sized openings for various sizes of boot.

Index